THE PLANETS

BY HOLLY DUHIG

©2017
Book Life
King's Lynn
Norfolk PE30 4LS

ISBN: 978-1-78637-201-7

Written by:
Holly Duhig
Edited by:
Charlie Ogden
Designed by:
Danielle Rippengill

A catalogue record for this book
is available from the British Library

PHOTO CREDITS

Abbreviations: l-left, r-right, b-bottom, t-top, c-centre, m-middle.

Front cover – Vadim Sadovski. Back cover – suns07butterfly. 2 – jassada watt_. 4–5 – Natalia80, 4l – Triff, 4ml – bluecrayola, 4m – Vadim Sadovski, 4mr – Nadalina, 4r – Kristina Shevchenko. 5tl – Vadim Sadovski, 5tr – Vadim Sadovski, 5ml – Tristan3D, 5mJ – Tristan3D, 5m – Vadim Sadovski, 5mr – Ksanawo, 5br – TuiPhotoEngineer. 6 – Stefano Garau, 6bl – Alex Mit, 6br – REDPIXEL.PL. 7 – Maria Starovoytova. 8 – Natalia80, 8tl – bluecrayola, 8tm – Vadim Sadovski, 8m – Nadalina, 8mr – Kristina Shevchenko, 8bl – Tristan3D, 8bm – Tristan3D, 8bm – Vadim Sadovski, 8br – Ksanawo. 9 – Vadim Sadovski. 11t – sdecoret, 11l – CVADRAT, 11r – HelenField, 11b – sdecoret. 12 – Giordano Aita. 13t – sdecoret, 13m – Vadim Sadovski, 13b – sdecoret. 14 – Webspark. 15t – sdecoret, 15m – muratart, 15b – sdecoret. 16l – Nostalgia for Infinity, 16r – NASA, modifications by Seddon [Public domain], via Wikimedia Commons. 17t – sdecoret, 17m – Vadim Sadovski, 17b – sdecoret. 18 – Paul Fleet. 19t – sdecoret, 19l – Nostalgia for Infinity, 19r – Nostalgia for Infinity, 19b – sdecoret. 20 – Tristan3D. 21t – sdecoret, 21m – Ksanawo, 21b – sdecoret. 22tr – iryna1, 22 – AvDe. 23t – sdecoret, 23m – MarcelClemens, 23b – sdecoret. 24 – SahonDesign. 25t – sdecoret, 25m – Vadim Sadovski, 25b – sdecoret. 27t – sdecoret, 27m – Tristan3D, 27b – sdecoret. 28 – acharyahargreaves. 29 – Yudin Andrii, 29 – adike. 30t – sdecoret, 30m – FrameAngel, 30b – sdecoret.

Images are courtesy of Shutterstock.com. With thanks to Getty Images, Thinkstock Photo and iStockphoto.

CONTENTS

Words that look like are explained in the glossary on page 31.

THE SOLAR SYSTEM

Our Solar System is made up of one star, eight planets, over one hundred moons and thousands of asteroids that zoom around, crashing into one another. The star at the centre of our Solar System is known as the Sun and the planets that orbit it are Mercury, Venus, Earth, Mars, Jupiter, Saturn, Uranus and Neptune. Mercury is the closest to the Sun and Neptune is the farthest away.

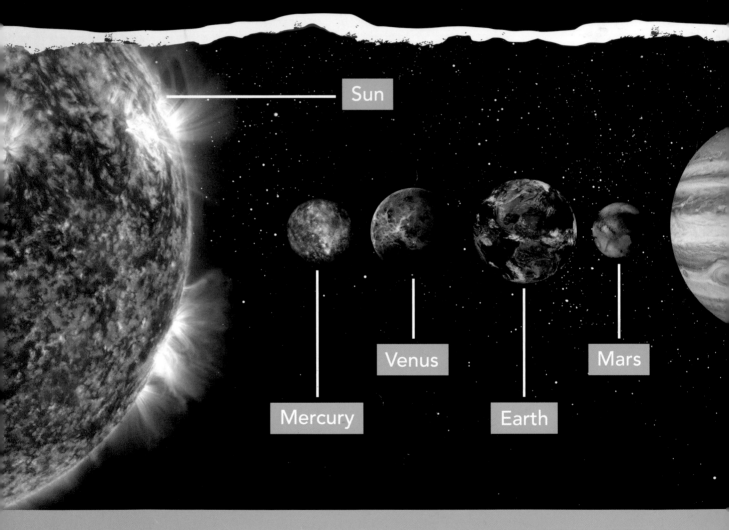

Sun

Venus

Mars

Mercury

Earth

All of the planets orbit the Sun at different speeds. The planets closer to the Sun take less time to go all the way round it than those farther away. Our planet takes about 365 days to orbit the Sun. This is called a year. Planets also spin round as they orbit the Sun. Our planet takes 24 hours to do a full turn. This is called a day.

Mercury:
4,900 km

Ganymede:
5,268 km

As well as planets, our Solar System is home to many moons. While moons are always smaller than the planets they orbit, they can be larger than other planets in the Solar System. For example, Ganymede, one of Jupiter's moons, is bigger than Mercury.

Neptune

Uranus

Saturn

Jupiter

Not all planets have moons. Mercury and Venus have none and Earth is the only planet in our Solar System to have just one moon. Bigger planets tend to have more moons. Jupiter, the biggest planet in our Solar System, has 67 confirmed moons!

WHERE IS OUR SOLAR SYSTEM?

Our Solar System is part of a galaxy called the Milky Way. A galaxy is a cluster of many solar systems, stars and planets that are held together by gravity and orbit around a black hole. There are billions of galaxies in the universe.

Milky Way

Black Hole

The Milky Way is about 100,000 light-years wide and is shaped like a big spiral. A light-year is a measurement based on how far light travels in a year. Scientists use light-years to measure the distance between objects in space because they can be extremely far away from each other. One light-year is 9.5 trillion kilometres!

Our own Solar System can be found about 30,000 light-years away from the Milky Way's centre. The Milky Way contains hundreds of other solar systems besides our own.

Our Solar System formed 4.6 billion years ago and is very special because, as far as we know, it is the only one that has life. But there could be life in other solar systems in the Milky Way or even other galaxies in the universe.

TYPES OF PLANET

There are two main types of planet in our Solar System. The first type are called terrestrial planets and the second type are called gas giants. Terrestrial planets are made of rock whereas gas giants are made of gas.

Terrestrial Planets

Gas Giants

All the planets, except Earth, are named after gods from Greek and Roman *mythology*.

The first four planets in the Solar System are terrestrial planets. This means they are made of rock. Mercury, Venus, Earth and Mars are all terrestrial planets. The rest of the planets, Jupiter, Saturn, Uranus and Neptune, are all made of gas that has been pulled together by gravity.

DWARF PLANETS

Dwarf planets are another type of planet. They tend to be much smaller and, because of this, they have much weaker gravity. This means that, when the Solar System was being formed, they were unable to pull all the nearby rocks and gases towards them. This has left the space around dwarf planets very cluttered.

Scientists used to think Pluto was the ninth planet in our Solar System, but in 2006 it was decided that Pluto was a dwarf planet.

The surface of Pluto has a love heart on it.

Pluto, Ceres, Haumea, Makemake and Eris are all the dwarf planets found in our Solar System so far, but scientists expect to find hundreds more. The moons of dwarf planets are often not much smaller than the dwarf planets they orbit. Pluto has five moons and its largest is about half as wide as Pluto itself.

MERCURY

Mercury is the closest planet to the Sun and the smallest planet in the Solar System. It has a very thin atmosphere. An atmosphere is a layer of gas that surrounds an object in space and traps heat. A thick atmosphere will keep the whole planet warm – including the side that isn't facing the Sun. A thin atmosphere, like Mercury's, will let the heat out, making one half of the planet very cold.

Mercury spins very slowly, making days and nights very long. This means one side is facing the Sun for a very long time, while the other is left in the freezing cold shade. Because of Mercury's thin atmosphere, the side not facing the Sun gets very cold very quickly.

Mercury can reach temperatures of 427 °C during the day, but at night it can drop to –180 °C.

Mercury's biggest crater is called the Caloris Basin and is 1,550 kilometres wide.

A thick atmosphere can also protect a planet from being hit by *meteorites* by crushing and burning them up before they hit the planet's surface. Mercury's thin atmosphere cannot properly protect it, which is why the planet is covered in lots of craters.

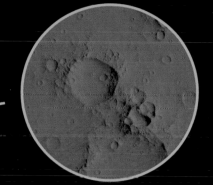

FACT FILE

NAME: Mercury
PLANET NUMBER: 1
DISTANCE FROM SUN: 58 million kilometres
DIAMETER: 4,900 kilometres
NUMBER OF MOONS: 0
ONE YEAR = 88 Earth days
ONE DAY = 59 Earth days

VENUS

Even though Venus is the second planet from the Sun, it is actually the hottest planet in our Solar System. This is because, unlike Mercury, Venus has a very thick atmosphere that traps a lot of heat. If you were to go to Venus, being under the weight of the planet's atmosphere would feel the same as swimming 1,000 kilometres deep in the ocean!

Earth is only 652 kilometres wider than Venus.

This thick atmosphere protects the planet by crushing and burning up any asteroids, comets and even space *probes* that enter it. Russia was the first country to successfully land a space probe on Venus, but it was quickly destroyed by the planet's heat. In many ways, Earth and Venus are very similar. They are a similar size and, like Earth, Venus used to have big chunks of land surrounded by seas. Venus is the closest planet to Earth and it is the brightest object in our nightsky, apart from the Moon, which has led to it being nicknamed 'morning star' or 'evening star'.

FACT FILE

NAME: Venus

PLANET NUMBER: 2

DISTANCE FROM SUN: 108 million kilometres

DIAMETER: 12,100 kilometres

NUMBER OF MOONS: 0

ONE YEAR = 225 Earth days

ONE DAY = 116 Earth days

EARTH

Our home is the third planet from the Sun. It is the only planet in our Solar System that can support life. This is because it has plenty of water and a thick atmosphere. Our atmosphere also has lots of **oxygen**, which humans and animals need in order to breathe.

Crust

Mantle

Outer Core

Inner Core

Although our atmosphere is perfect for life now, it may not always be this way. This is because humans pollute the atmosphere with toxic gases from things like factories, cars and aeroplanes. These gases, like those in Venus's atmosphere, trap heat in the planet and might make the Earth too hot to live on.

Planet Earth is made of many layers. Its inner core is made of a mixture of metals like iron and nickel. The core can reach temperatures of 6,000 °C! Covering this is a layer of liquid metal. Beyond that is the mantle, which is covered in a rocky crust.

FACT FILE

NAME: Earth
PLANET NUMBER: 3
DISTANCE FROM SUN: 150 million kilometres
DIAMETER: 12,756 kilometres
NUMBER OF MOONS: 1
ONE YEAR = 365.25 days
ONE DAY = 24 hours

MARS

Mars's landscape is a lot like Earth's. It has canyons and mountains as well as polar ice caps. Mars is also known for having lots of volcanoes and is home to the biggest volcano in the Solar System, Olympus Mons.

Olympus Mons is about the same size as the US state of Arizona!

Humans have already made it to the Moon and Mars is the next object in the night sky that we have set our sights on! We have landed spacecraft on Mars to gather information but, so far, no human has set foot on it. It would take an *astronaut* about six months to get there in a rocket.

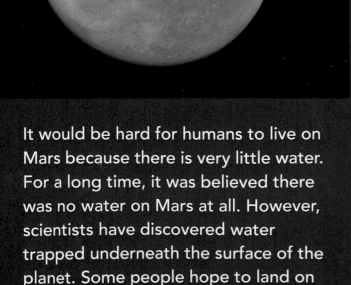

It would be hard for humans to live on Mars because there is very little water. For a long time, it was believed there was no water on Mars at all. However, scientists have discovered water trapped underneath the surface of the planet. Some people hope to land on Mars and begin trying to make it a safe place for humans to live. At the moment, Mars's thin atmosphere doesn't have enough oxygen for humans to breathe. This thin atmosphere also doesn't trap much of the Sun's heat, so Mars would be very cold at night!

FACT FILE

NAME: Mars

PLANET NUMBER: 4

DISTANCE FROM SUN: 228 million kilometres

DIAMETER: 6,792 kilometres

NUMBER OF MOONS: 2

ONE YEAR: 687 Earth days

ONE DAY: 24 Earth hours

ASTEROID BELT

The asteroid belt is not a planet, but it is an important part of our Solar System. It orbits the Sun between Mars and Jupiter. It is made up of millions of pieces of rock that range in size from a grain of sand to over 400 kilometres wide! Although the asteroids in the asteroid belt are often believed to be close together, they are in fact hundreds, or even thousands, of kilometres apart.

The asteroid belt is home to the 950-kilometre-wide dwarf planet Ceres! Scientists recently discovered that Ceres has lots of ice under its surface. This means it might have once been home to living things.

CERES

Ceres is the smallest dwarf
planet in the Solar System. It
only takes nine hours to rotate.

It also has one big mountain
called Ahuna Mons.

JUPITER

Jupiter is the biggest planet in the Solar System and the first of the gas giants. It is often called the Red Giant because of its size. Jupiter's width is equal to 11 Earth-sized planets side-by-side.

The red spot on Jupiter's side is a gigantic storm which is roughly the size of Earth!

Because of its size, Jupiter has very strong gravity.
It has been able to pull many objects towards it, which is why it has 67 moons!
Scientists think that Jupiter acts like a giant vacuum cleaner for the Solar System by sucking in passing meteoroids with its gravity before they reach the other planets.

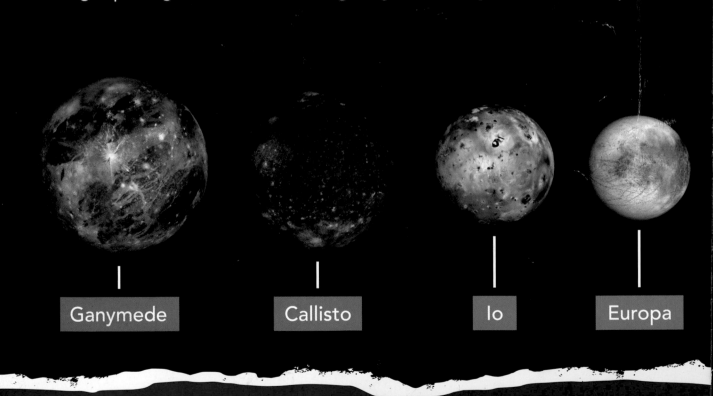

Ganymede

Callisto

Io

Europa

Jupiter's rotation is much faster than Earth's – its days are only ten hours long. The speed of this rotation means the clouds of gas in its atmosphere form long belts and make the planet look stripy. These belts of gas move very quickly, which often causes storms on the planet.

FACT FILE

NAME: Jupiter
PLANET NUMBER: 5
DISTANCE FROM SUN: 779 million kilometres
DIAMETER: 142,984 kilometres
NUMBER OF MOONS: 67
ONE YEAR = 11.86 Earth years
ONE DAY = 10 Earth hours

SATURN

Saturn is a gas planet that also has a rocky centre. Even though the outer temperature of Saturn can drop to −178 °C, its inner core may reach temperatures as hot as the surface of the Sun!

Saturn is famous for the rings which orbit it. These rings are made of chunks of ice. Scientists think they might have been formed when one of Saturn's moons was broken apart by the strength of the planet's gravity.

Galileo Galilei

The Italian astronomer, Galileo Galilei, was the first person to observe Saturn through a **telescope**. On his first observation, he did not see Saturn's rings. This is because Galileo was looking at them head-on, so only a small sliver of the rings could be seen. Later, when the planet had moved and tilted slightly, he was able to see the rings. This is the same effect that would happen if you held a piece of paper flat at eye level. You would only see a thin white line, but if you tilted it forwards or backwards, you would be able to see much more of it.

FACT FILE

NAME: Saturn

PLANET NUMBER: 6

DISTANCE FROM SUN: 1,427 million kilometres

DIAMETER: 120,536 kilometres

NUMBER OF MOONS: 62

ONE YEAR = 29.7 Earth years

ONE DAY = 10.7 Earth hours

URANUS

Uranus is made of the gases hydrogen and methane. Methane is responsible for many of the planet's interesting features, including its blue colour and diamond rain. That's right! While diamonds are considered precious on Earth, scientists think it rains diamonds on Uranus. The planet's lightning storms turn the methane into soot. As this soot falls from the sky, it is crushed into diamonds by the weight of the atmosphere.

Unlike the other planets, Uranus spins on its side like a barrel rolling along the ground. Scientists have two ideas as to why this is. The first is that, at some point, a large object struck the planet with such force that it tilted onto its side. The second idea is that, when the Solar System was still young, one of Uranus's moons was pulled away from the planet by an object with stronger gravity. As this moon moved farther away, Uranus tilted towards it until it was on its side.

FACT FILE

NAME: Uranus
PLANET NUMBER: 7
DISTANCE FROM SUN: 2,871 million kilometres
DIAMETER: 51,118 kilometres
NUMBER OF MOONS: 27
ONE YEAR = 84 Earth years
ONE DAY = 17.2 Earth hours

NEPTUNE

Neptune wasn't discovered until 1846 and it is the farthest planet from the Sun. Because it is so far away, Neptune takes 165 years to orbit the Sun. This means that it has only completed one full orbit since its discovery.

The Great Dark Spot

The Scooter

Neptune has 14 moons and its biggest is called Triton. Triton is the coldest place in our Solar System.

Out of all the planets, Neptune experiences the most extreme weather. The wind travels in a different direction to the rotation of the planet, which causes huge storms. One of these storms is called The Great Dark Spot, which has winds that travel up to 2,400 kilometres an hour! Another storm on Neptune is called The Scooter. The Scooter is a group of clouds that whip round the planet every 16 hours.

FACT FILE

NAME: Neptune
PLANET NUMBER: 8
DISTANCE FROM SUN: 4,498 million kilometres
DIAMETER: 49,244 kilometres
NUMBER OF MOONS: 14
ONE YEAR = 165 Earth years
ONE DAY = 16.1 Earth hours

LIFE ON OTHER PLANETS

Aliens are often the subject of books and films, but could there really be life on other planets? The famous scientist Stephen Hawking believes aliens are out there somewhere, but doesn't think we should try to contact them. After all, they might be dangerous! What do you think? Will we ever find aliens on other planets? Is it a good idea to look for them?

Scientists are always on the lookout for planets that might be able to support life. They search for planets that have water, are not too close or too far away from a star and have an atmosphere that's not too thick or too thin.

Plenty of moons and planets in our Solar System are contenders in the race to find alien life. This includes Jupiter, Uranus and Mars, because they all have water on them. Humans have been looking for signs of life on Mars since the 1800s. However, if these planets do have life, it will probably be microscopic. We must look beyond the planets in our own Solar System if we ever hope to find more advanced alien life.

Where do you think aliens are hiding?
Close to home or far away?
Will they be really big or really small?

QUICK QUIZ

What is the biggest crater on Mercury called?

Why is Venus the hottest planet?

How many layers are there to planet Earth?

How long would it take for an astronaut to get to Mars in a spacecraft?

How many moons does Jupiter have?

What is Jupiter's red spot?

Who was the first person to look at Saturn through a telescope?

What is different about Uranus's rotation?

What are the names of both of the big storms on the surface of Neptune?

Which famous scientist believes aliens exist?

GLOSSARY

°C	the symbol for degrees Celsius, the metric measurement of temperature
ALIENS	extra-terrestrial life
ASTEROIDS	rocky and irregularly shaped objects that orbit around the Sun
ASTRONAUT	a person who is trained to travel in spacecraft
DIAMETER	the distance through the centre of an object
GRAVITY	the force that attracts physical bodies together and increases in strength as a body's mass increases
MANTLE	a layer of the Earth made up of semi-molten rock
METEORITES	a piece of rock that successfully enters a planet's atmosphere without being destroyed
METEOROID	a piece of rock in space that is yet to enter a planet's atmosphere
MICROSCOPIC	so small it can only be viewed under a microscope
MOONS	natural satellites that orbit a planet
MYTHOLOGY	collections of stories that belong to a particular culture
ORBIT	the path that an object makes around a larger object in space
OXYGEN	a natural gas that all living things need in order to survive
PROBES	types of spacecraft designed to explore other planets and send back information
ROTATE	turn around a central point or axis
STAR	giant ball of hot gas in space
TELESCOPE	a tool used to view distant objects

INDEX